FRANZ SCHUBERT

COMPLETE CHAMBER MUSIC FOR STRINGS

Edited by

Eusebius Mandyczewski and Joseph Hellmesberger

FROM THE BREITKOPF & HÄRTEL
COMPLETE WORKS EDITION

DOVER PUBLICATIONS, INC., NEW YORK

Contents

(The Quintet and Trios are edited by Eusebius Mandyczewski; the Quartets, by Joseph Hellmesberger and Mandyczewski. The dates in parentheses are the years of composition.)

Published in Canada by General Publishing Company, Ltd.,
30 Lesmill Road, Don Mills, Toronto, Ontario.
Published in the United Kingdom by Constable and Company, Ltd.,
10 Orange Street, London WC 2.

This Dover edition, first published in 1973, is an unabridged and unaltered republication of the following sections of *Franz Schubert's Werke. Kritisch durchgesehene Gesammtausgabe,* originally published by Breitkopf & Härtel in Leipzig:
Series 4 (dated 1890): *Quintett für Streichinstrumente* (complete).
Series 5 (1890): *Quartette für Streichinstrumente* (complete).
Series 6 (1890): *Trio für Streichinstrumente* (complete).
Pages 93–105 of Series 21 (1897): *Supplement* (the additional trio).

International Standard Book Number: 0-486-21463-X
Library of Congress Catalog Card Number: 72-80718

Manufactured in the United States of America
Dover Publications, Inc.
180 Varick Street
New York, N.Y. 10014

Quintet in C Major, Op. 163

4

SCHERZO.
Presto.

Trio.
Andante sostenuto.

Tempo I.

Scherzo **D. C.**

Allegretto.

37

41

Più allegro.

43

Quartet No. 1

MENUETTO.

51

Quartet No. 2 in C Major

56

MENUETTO.
Allegro.

Trio.

Quartet No. 3 in B-flat Major

MENUETTO.
Allegro ma non troppo.

73

Quartet No. 4 in C Major

Andante con moto.

(6. März 1813.)

MENUETTO.
Allegro.

Men. D. C.

93

Quartet No. 5 in B-flat Major

Allegro.

106

111

Quartet No. 6 in D Major

MENUETTO.

Allegro.

Allegro.

Quartet No. 7 in D Major

MENUETTO.
Allegretto.

Presto.

149

Quartet No. 8 in B-flat Major, Op. 168

157

158

In 4½ Stunden verfertigt.

Andante sostenuto. (6. Sept. 1814.)

160

MENUETTO.
Allegro.

(10. Sept. 1814.)

165

Trio.

Quartet No. 9 in G Minor

MENUETTO.
Allegro vivace.

185

Quartet No. 10 in E-flat Major, Op. 125 No. 1

SCHERZO.
Prestissimo.

Adagio.

200

Allegro.

208

Quartet No. 11 in E Major, Op. 125 No. 2

MENUETTO.
Allegro vivace.

RONDO.
Allegro vivace.

Men. D. C.

Quartet No. 12 (Quartett-Satz) in C Minor

228

Quartet No. 13 in A Minor, Op. 29

239

246

MENUETTO.

Allegretto.

Trio.

Men. D.C.

Quartet No. 14 in D Minor ("Death and the Maiden")

265

269

Andante con moto.

273

276

SCHERZO.
Allegro molto.

Scherzo da Capo.

Presto.

286

288

290

292

Prestissimo.

Quartet No. 15 in G Major, Op. 161

302

308

310

SCHERZO.
Allegro vivace.

314

Trio.
Allegretto.

Scherzo da Capo.

Allegro assai.

319

Trio in B-flat Major

Trio in B-flat Major

Andante.

Menuetto.
Allegretto.

Trio.

Menuetto da capo.

Rondo.
Allegretto.